HEALTHCARE HEROES

How Therapy Dogs Change Lives!

Dedication

This book is dedicated to all the volunteer pet therapy teams and healthcare professionals who have incorporated animal assisted interventions into their practice. The service you and your canine companion provide truly changes the lives of others, and it is a gift that we hope others will be inspired to give after reading this book.

Together, we can make a difference!

About the Authors

Christi Williams is a physical therapist who fell in love with animal assisted therapy after training her dog, Layla, to be a registered therapy animal. Christi's mission of educating people of all ages on the benefits of therapy animals came about after several years of witnessing the positive impact that Layla's visits had on others. Her goal is to inspire others to volunteer with their dog, so that more people will experience the benefit of working with a therapy animal in the future.

Angela Bozik is an occupational therapist who helped author this book as part of her capstone project for her doctoral degree in occupational therapy. She is currently training her dog, Maisy, to be a registered therapy animal in the future. As an occupational therapist, Angela is passionate about helping children reach their fullest potential and hopes to use animal assisted therapy in her future practice. Her goal is to teach others about the power of therapy animals in our lives.

Healthcare Heroes

ISBN: 979-8-9869577-0-8

Cover and interior design by Simon Thompson.

Table of Contents

What is a Therapy Dog?

Dogs are often known as man's best friend; however, dogs can be so much more than that! Many people have dogs as pets, but did you know that you can train and register your dog to become a therapy dog? A registered therapy dog team consists of a well-behaved dog and their owner, or handler, who have completed general obedience training as well as a therapy dog course. As a team, they are then required to pass an in-person evaluation with an established therapy animal organization. Therapy dogs can be any breed if they are friendly, calm, enjoy interacting with others, and are comfortable being in a wide variety of settings.

As a team, the handler and the therapy dog volunteer to visit with people of all ages to help decrease stress and anxiety and increase happiness. Some dogs may help people work on certain activities to improve physical strength, while others help with more emotional support. No matter where you meet a therapy dog, their main job is to bring joy and comfort to those in need.

Layla the "Rehab Lab"

DID YOU KNOW?

THERE ARE OVER 50,000 REGISTERED THERAPY DOG TEAMS IN THE UNITED STATES.

Therapy Dog Story:

Layla the Superhero

I always knew Layla was a special dog. She has a gentle disposition, a calming presence, ears that are soft as velvet, and the sweetest big brown eyes. Layla is a yellow Labrador Retriever who became a registered therapy dog when she was five years old. To be completely honest, I had no idea what kind of impact Layla would have on others. I simply thought it would be fun to share her sweet soul with patients in various healthcare settings.

As we began training to become a registered therapy dog team, we participated in a fundraising event for a young boy with Duchenne Muscular Dystrophy. There was a superhero theme for the event, so Layla came dressed in her superhero outfit to support young Garrett – the REAL hero of the event. It was a fun day, and Layla even won a medal that was awarded by Garrett himself. ▶

We later received a very special drawing from Garrett showing that Layla served as *his* hero that day! That was the moment when I realized that a therapy dog visit was so much more than simply petting a dog. A visit with a therapy dog meant HOPE for some

6

people. For others, a therapy dog visit gave them the necessary COURAGE they needed in that moment. And for many, a therapy dog visit provided REASSURANCE in a time of uncertainty.

We will never know the full extent of the impact a therapy dog visit has on others. What we do know, however, is that the impact of these visits is profound. And at times, they are even life changing. Being a hero for the day is where Layla's journey began. And it only got better from there.

Story told by therapy dog team Christi & Layla

Therapy Dogs in Healthcare

Therapy dogs are becoming more and more popular in a variety of healthcare settings, such as hospitals, doctor's offices, and therapy clinics, because they have such a positive influence on both patients and healthcare professionals. Having a loved one in the hospital or going to see a doctor when not feeling well can be a stressful experience.

Having a therapy dog in these settings can help to ease patient's nerves and make these appointments a little more enjoyable.

DID YOU KNOW?

INTERACTING WITH A DOG CAN ACTUALLY INCREASE THE HORMONE OXYTOCIN IN OUR BRAINS. THIS HORMONE IS SOMETIMES CALLED THE "LOVE HORMONE" AND CAN PLAY A ROLE IN REDUCING STRESS AND ANXIETY.

Therapy Dog versus Facility Dog

Therapy Dogs:

Many hospitals and medical facilities request to have therapy dog teams visit their patients and staff throughout the week. These teams volunteer their time to visit with those who need some extra love from a happy dog. Once the team has completed and passed all the requirements and are registered through a therapy dog organization, they can visit with patients when given permission from the facility.

Facility Dogs:

Some hospitals or medical facilities hire full-time facility dogs to be part of their staff. Facility dogs are a special type of service dog trained by outside service organizations to be working dogs. These dogs are trained to do many different tasks. Since these dogs work full time at a facility, there will always be a four-legged friend nearby wagging their tail and showing everyone they meet love and affection.

Physical therapist, Chrissy, and facility dog, Norman, working on balance activities with a patient

Rehabilitation Facility

A rehabilitation facility is a place where patients go to work on the skills they need to return home independently after an injury or major illness. Therapy dogs can be used in these facilities to assist occupational therapists, physical therapists, or even speech therapists during their treatment sessions. In this type of setting, therapy dogs can help to increase motivation and participation. They have even been known to help people feel less pain when they are working on various physical activities.

DID YOU KNOW?

RESEARCH STUDIES HAVE FOUND THAT INDIVIDUALS FEEL LESS PAIN WHEN ANIMALS ARE INVOLVED IN THEIR THERAPY SESSIONS. THIS IS BECAUSE THE ANIMAL MAY DISTRACT THE PATIENT FROM THEIR PAIN OR HELP TO INCREASE THEIR ENGAGEMENT IN THE EXERCISES MAKING THEM FOCUS ON SOMETHING ELSE.

Therapy Dog Story:

Layla the Rehab Lab

Layla attended a summer camp for kids with various disabilities that cause one side of their body to become weaker. At this camp, the goal was to have the kids use their weaker arm to do fun activities to improve their strength and control. To do this, a temporary cast was placed on their stronger arm so they could not use that side for the activities. On the first day of camp, kids were often frustrated when trying to use their weak arm for the tasks, but then Layla showed up and everything changed!

Instead of feeling embarrassed or frustrated with their disability, the kids couldn't wait to pick up Layla's pink tennis ball and practice throwing it to her so she could jump up and catch it! The activity was fun and because Layla was there to play with them, the kids quickly forgot they were using their weak side, and their confidence in trying this difficult task grew tremendously. Layla's visit was the highlight of the week!

Story told by therapy dog team Christi & Layla

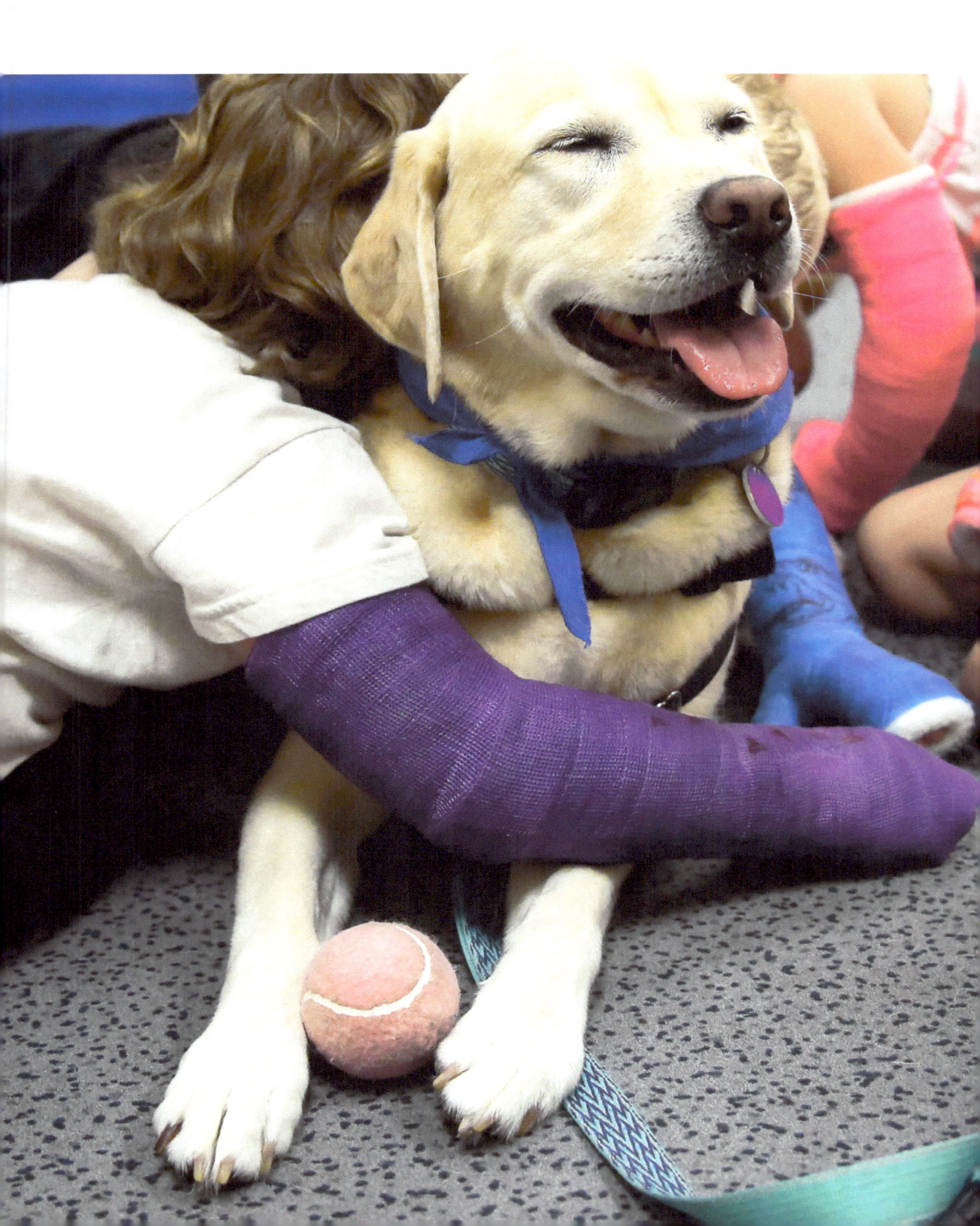

Lillie is working on balance and strengthening while brushing Tucker.

Occupational Therapy

Occupational therapy helps people return to doing the activities they need or want to do in their daily life. Using a therapy dog in occupational therapy settings can help patients work on daily living skills, such as brushing, feeding, or giving the dog water. They may also practice fine motor skills, such as working on buttoning or zipping up the dog's vest.

Some children do not like to touch certain textures.

One fun activity they can do to work on overcoming this is to make yummy dog treats. They can mix together oatmeal, peanut butter, and banana for their furry friend, and they may not even realize their hands are getting dirty! While some of these activities might not look like therapy, the therapist is always creating activities with a hidden skill. The therapy dog simply helps to make therapy more fun for the children, and it's fun for the dog, too!

Physical Therapy

In physical therapy, therapists design activities and exercises to help people regain their movement and strength.

Often times, physical therapists help their patients stretch different muscles throughout their body. Having a dog lay next to them can make these stretches go by a little faster. You may also see someone throwing a ball to the dog, which is a fun way to work on grasping and throwing skills.

Dogs can also help with balance and coordination activities such as standing on one leg when trying to kick a ball. Many times, people take therapy dogs for a walk during their therapy session. These walks are not just normal walks but are known as gait training. The dogs often help motivate the person to walk farther down the hall than usual.

Patient is petting Tucker while working on stretching activities.

Speech Therapy

Speech therapists help people with their communication skills. They can help people learn how to say certain words that may be difficult to pronounce. Having a dog in speech therapy is fun because the patient is able to talk to the dog instead of the therapist. The patient can give the dog commands, like telling him to sit, roll over, or fetch. This can help with practicing different speech sounds and words the patient is working on with their speech therapist.

Dogs can also help children learn how to read. Reading out loud to a therapy dog can help motivate children to try something that is difficult for them. They may find it is less stressful to read to a dog than reading to another person. Dogs are a great support team that do not judge how well the child is reading but are there to just listen to a fun story.

Hospital Settings

You may see therapy dogs walking down the halls of a loud hospital or stopping by each room to say hello. Hospitals can be a scary place, but all of the nurses and doctors are working hard to make people feel better.

The therapy dogs that visit hospitals are an important part of the team to help make people feel more comfortable during their stay. They may even jump up on the hospital bed for some extra love and cuddles. Getting a dog hug before a medical procedure can always help to make these procedures feel less scary!

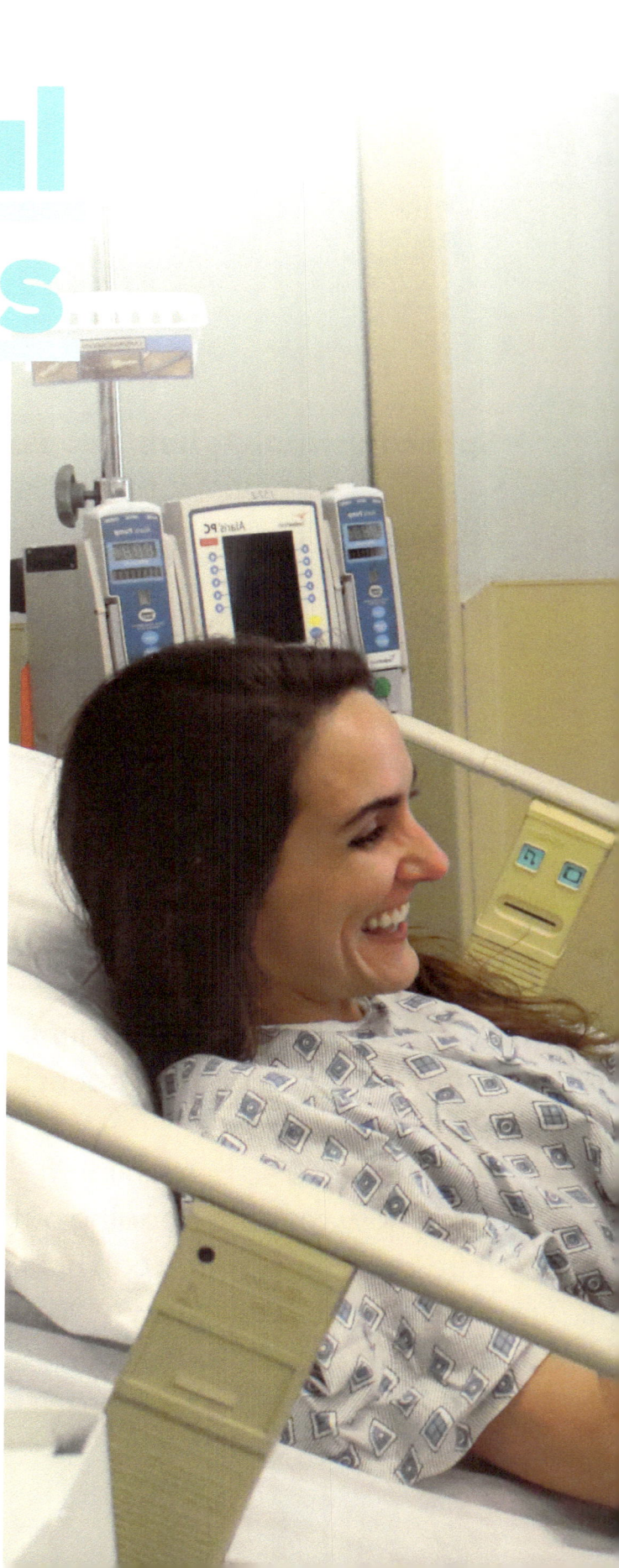

Michelle and therapy dog, Swoosh, love visiting with children in the oncology unit.

Oncology Clinics

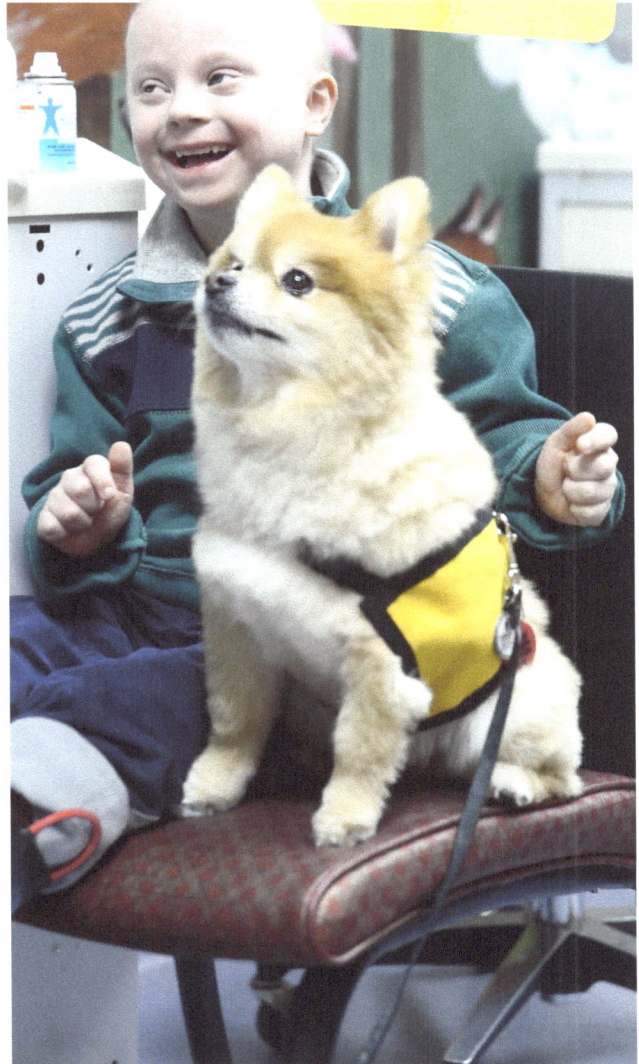

Therapy dogs sometimes wander into the oncology clinic in the hospital. The oncology clinic is where people receive chemotherapy to treat cancer. This can be a very long, boring, and sometimes painful process. Having therapy dogs there can help to make this process a little easier by visiting with each patient for a few minutes for some pets and snuggles. If the dog is small enough, they may even sit on the patient's lap. Therapy dogs love to show off their tricks and always appreciate a yummy treat from the patients they visit.

Therapy Dog Story:

Swoosh Comforts

In August 2014, we heard the words no parent wants to hear. "Your child has cancer." Mitchell was only four years old when he was diagnosed with Acute Lymphoblastic Leukemia (ALL). He was immediately admitted to the hospital for chemotherapy treatment that would last for three and a half years. While we were in the hospital, Mitchell was randomly selected to be in a study to show how therapy dogs could impact a child going through cancer treatments.

The sessions began at his first oncology appointment. Needless to say, walking into the oncology clinic for the very first time was quite overwhelming. It was a whole new world that we knew nothing about. We were all scared. The nurse came and got us from the waiting room and took us back to where Mitchell would be meeting Swoosh.

Mitchell was so scared and would not speak to anyone. Then the door opened, and the cutest, fluffiest dog named Swoosh came into the room. Mitchell immediately lit up. Honestly, we all did. ▶

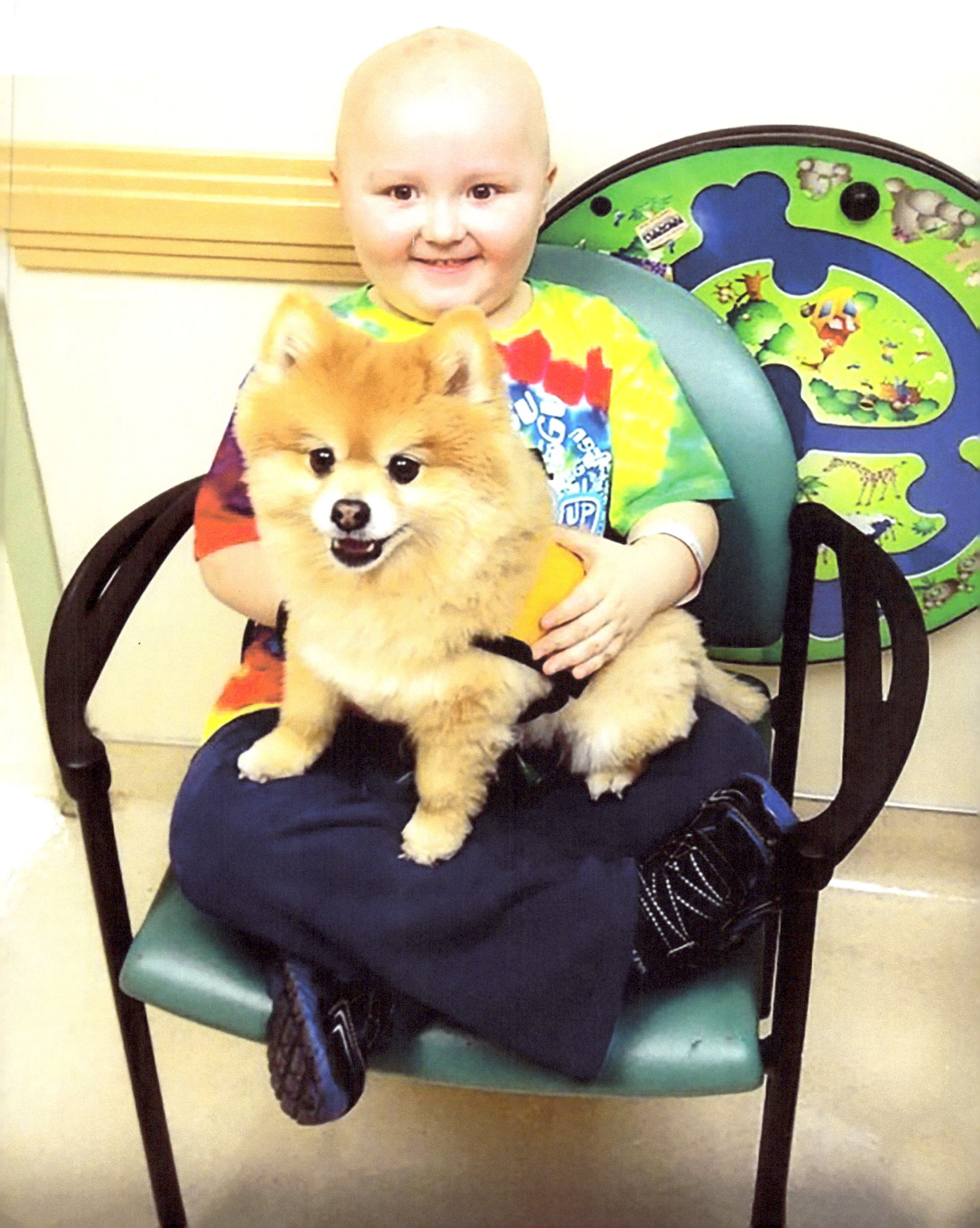

Mitchell got to pet and brush Swoosh and even feed him a few treats. Then he looked through Swoosh's photo album of him wearing cute costumes.

Mitchell still would not talk to anyone, but I could tell he enjoyed playing with Swoosh. After his 20 minutes were up, Swoosh left the room, and Mitchell got his chemotherapy treatment. The very next day, Mitchell asked me when he would get to go back to the clinic to get chemotherapy so he could see his new best friend, Swoosh.

Over time not only did Mitchell develop a wonderful relationship with Swoosh, but so did the rest of our family. Swoosh became a therapy dog for our entire family. He brought so much joy and

happiness to us in the 20 minutes we got to spend with him before Mitchell's chemotherapy treatments that it overshadowed the fear we all felt. Swoosh helped Mitchell to feel comfortable and safe and take his mind off of why he was at the oncology clinic. That helped my husband and I so much because Mitchell actually enjoyed going to the clinic to see his best friend, Swoosh. Story told by Mitchell's Mom, Kristy.

"SWOOSH WAS THE ABSOLUTE BEST THING THAT COULD HAVE HAPPENED AT THE WORST TIME OF OUR LIFE."
-KRISTY (MITCHELL'S MOM)

Healthcare Professionals

While therapy dogs in healthcare settings help a lot of patients, they also have an important role in helping the healthcare professionals, too! That's right, even the doctors, nurses, and staff members at hospitals or other medical facilities love to see therapy dogs during their day. Healthcare professionals are often very busy checking in on patients, doing paperwork, and talking to families. There are days when they can feel very overwhelmed. Taking a minute to pet a therapy dog allows them a chance to reset and recharge for the rest of their day. Some even keep treats at their desks to make sure the dogs come visit them, too!

"THERAPY DOGS BREAK UP HARD DAYS WITH A RAY OF SUNSHINE. THERE IS NOTHING THAT LIFTS YOUR SPIRIT QUITE LIKE THE PRESENCE OF A DOG."
-EMERGENCY DEPARTMENT STAFF MEMBER

Day, RN, BSN
Women's Health
Registered Nurse 2, VPNPP

Tucker is visiting with a family in the waiting room

Families of Patients

It is important to not forget about the families who are waiting for their loved ones in the waiting room. This can be a very scary and stressful time waiting for updates on how their loved one is doing. Some families may be waiting for hours and others just a few minutes, but they all need a little extra love during this difficult time. Therapy dogs sometimes walk through the waiting room to help these families feel less stressed and to take their mind off of worrying for just one moment.

Dental Offices

Going to the dentist can cause anxiety for some patients. Sometimes people need a lot of dental work done that can be uncomfortable and very noisy. However, a visit from a therapy dog can help make everything better!

Therapy dogs in dental offices can be trained to lay their head on the patient's lap throughout a dental procedure, so that the patient can focus on petting the dog rather than focusing on the procedure itself.

Other times, a therapy dog may even lay on the patient's lap, which is similar to a weighted blanket. The pressure from the weight of the dog creates a calming effect, which further helps reduce patient anxiety.

Having a therapy dog present during a dental visit makes teeth cleaning appointments go by a lot faster, too!

"MY PRACTICE WOULD NOT BE THE SAME WITHOUT BODIE'S PRESENCE. HIS ABILITY TO CALM OUR PATIENTS AND MAKE THEM FEEL COMFORTABLE IS IRREPLACEABLE. SOME CHILDREN WON'T EVEN COME TO THE DENTIST WITHOUT KNOWING BODIE WILL BE HERE."

DR. WILL

Therapy dog, Bodie, comforting a patient while at the dentist. When patients want Bodie to lay on their lap, they grab a blanket, say "cuddles," and he is ready for a nap.

Skilled Nursing Facilities

Outside of rehabilitation facilities and hospitals, many elderly patients living in a skilled nursing facility also love a good visit with a therapy dog. Patients at these facilities don't need to be in a hospital, but they are not ready to take care of themselves alone at home. Therapy dogs visit from room to room in skilled nursing facilities bringing comfort and companionship to each patient.

Residents in these facilities sometimes feel lonely because they are away from their home and family. Therapy dog visits can help improve socialization and help people feel less lonely during their stay. They can also be a little reminder of their loving pets at home. Therapy dog visits can help to break up the day-to-day routine and be something patients look forward to each week.

DID YOU KNOW?

DOGS CAN HELP TO IMPROVE SOCIAL INTERACTIONS IN ELDERLY PATIENTS AND CAN BE A FRIEND OR COMPANION FOR THEM WHEN OTHER HUMANS ARE NOT AROUND. SOMETIMES PATIENTS WILL EVEN TALK TO THE DOGS WHEN THEY HAVE NEVER TALKED TO THE STAFF OR OTHER PATIENTS BEFORE.

Therapy Dog Story:

Duncan Brings Out Happiness

Duncan is a rescue dog who is missing part of his jaw from cancer surgery, which often causes his tongue to hang out the side of his mouth. He has a floppy ear and the sweetest disposition.

During one of our visits with patients and staff, Duncan enjoyed his usual ear rubs, and I enjoyed a story told by an elderly lady as she snuggled his soft fur. Suddenly the room went quiet. Looking around, I noticed that a few of the nurses had tears in their eyes. I knew something touching had happened during that interaction. When the lady finished her story, I thanked her for her time, and Duncan went on to greet his next friend.

One of the nurses later explained to me that the lady we had been talking to had been a patient of theirs for quite a while and this was the first time the nurses ever heard her speak. In fact, they didn't think she was able to speak at all. It is times like this that I realize the true power of dogs in our lives.

Story told by therapy dog team Jenyfer & Duncan

DID YOU KNOW?

IT IS NOT UNCOMMON FOR A THERAPY DOG TO BE A RESCUE DOG, OR A DOG WITH A DISABILITY. THE MOST IMPORTANT THING TO CONSIDER IS THE DOG'S TEMPERAMENT AND DESIRE TO WORK.

Hospice

Hospice provides special care for patients in their last stage of life. The main goal is to provide care to help these individuals live the rest of their life as comfortably as possible.

Many family members experience grief or sadness during this difficult time. Having therapy dogs visit these patients and their families allows for some moments of comfort during this final stage of life. A simple tail wag can often bring joy and smiles to everyone in the room during an otherwise sad time.

"THE BEST PART ABOUT VISITING HOSPICE IS THE IMPACT THE DOGS HAVE ON THE STAFF, THE PATIENTS, AND EVEN MORE SO, THE FAMILIES. THEY ARE IN AN EMOTIONAL TWILIGHT ZONE, AND TO BE ABLE TO LAUGH AND PET THE DOGS AND REALLY SMILE, IS A GIFT."
VICKI & THERAPY DOG, BAYLEY

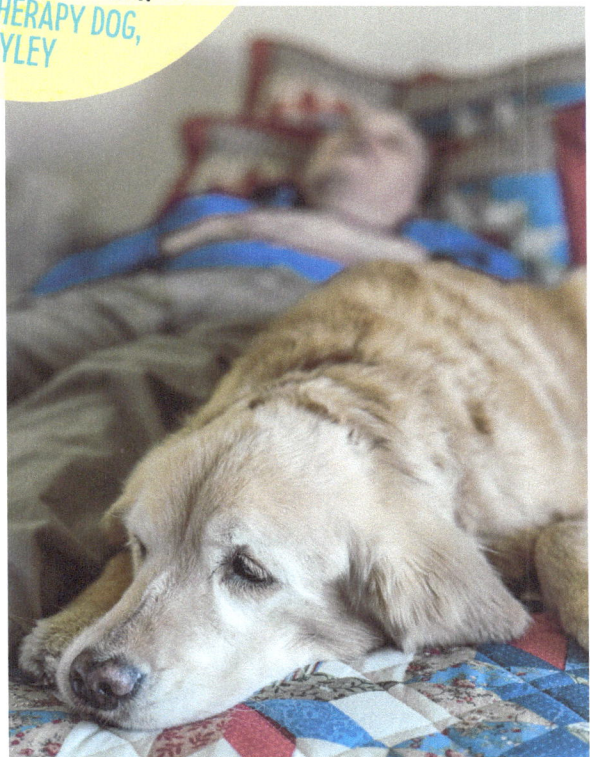

Mental Health Counseling

Everyone experiences some form of a mental health challenge at some point in their life, whether that is feeling stressed for an exam, sad during a funeral, or anxious while waiting for results from a doctor's appointment. These challenges can even be something more severe, such as depression or post-traumatic stress disorder that require mental health counseling. Therapy dogs can help patients feel more comfortable talking to their therapist about how they are feeling. The simple presence of a therapy dog can be enough to lift a person's mood and create a more positive environment.

DID YOU KNOW?

MANY CRISIS RESPONSE DOGS ARE THERAPY DOGS WHO HAVE BEEN SPECIALLY TRAINED TO HANDLE STRESSFUL SITUATIONS. THESE TEAMS TRAVEL TO PLACES FOLLOWING TRAUMATIC EVENTS TO HELP PEOPLE REMAIN CALM AND TO PROVIDE COMFORT AND ENCOURAGEMENT TO THOSE AFFECTED BY THE CRISIS.

Therapy dogs can bring a sense of comfort during mental health counseling sessions.

Therapy Dog Story:

Silver Comforts

Silver visited regularly at a day center for adults with brain injuries. Sillie, as we called her, was a bit of a diva who thought the therapy programs were designed specifically for people to show appreciation for her wonderfulness.

Walking into the center one day we heard loud screaming. All the clients were seated in the auditorium, quietly watching a movie, except for Joe. Joe was screaming and rocking in his seat. The staff members said he had been like this for hours and nothing brought him relief.

Silver's usual position was standing still, waiting for people to come to her, but this day she started pulling me over to the aisle where Joe sat. Curious to see what she was up to, we walked over to Joe. Silver stood next to him and

plopped her head in his lap. Joe did not seem to notice anything but his pain as he continued screaming and rocking. All of a sudden, he went still. Looking down at Sillie (whose big head was still in his lap), he wrapped his arms around her and began rocking again, but now he was quiet and had an expression of pure peace. Sillie and Joe stayed like this, rocking gently, for at least 15 minutes. After a while, visibly relieved, Joe stopped his movements, gave a happy smile, released his hold on Silver, and was able to enjoy the rest of the movie.

Story told by therapy dog team Jenyfer & Silver

Silver the therapy dog.

Maisy is training to be a therapy dog.

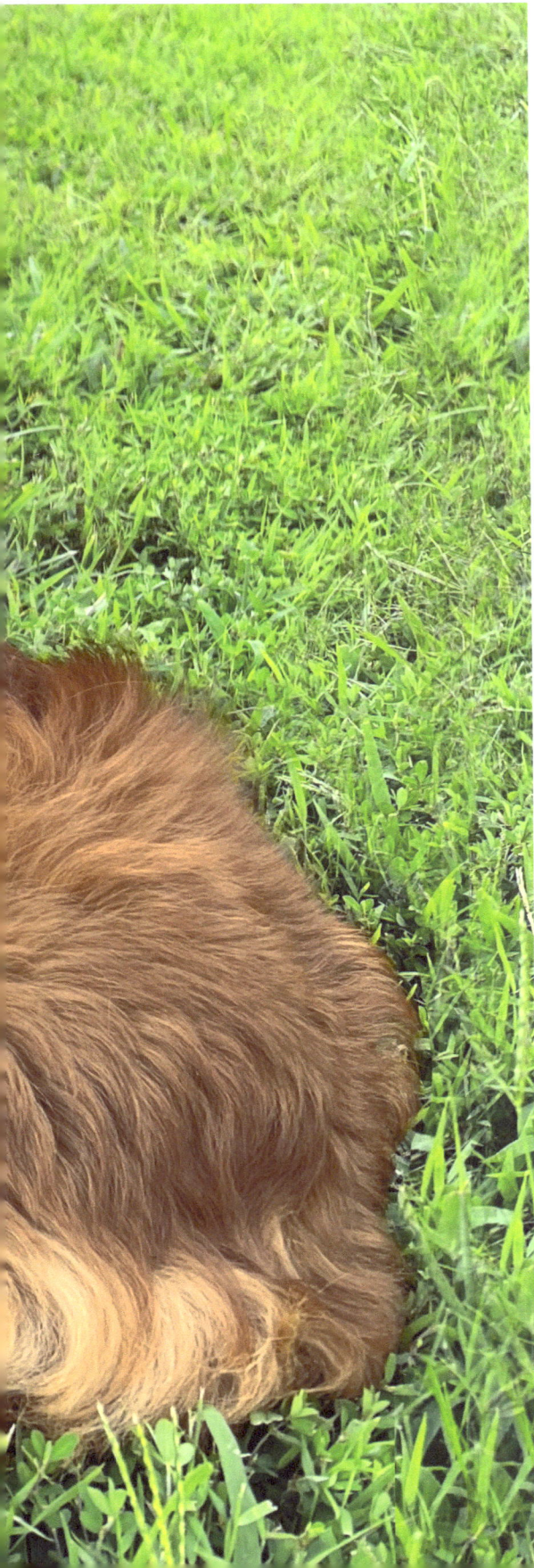

Future Therapy Dogs

Therapy dog teams also love to help train future therapy dogs by volunteering at training classes to help new teams become comfortable with a lot of different people and other dogs. They also help by spreading the word about the many benefits of pet therapy and inspire others to train and register their dog to become a therapy dog in the future.

Meet Some Real Teams

Christi & Layla

Christi is a physical therapist and professor at Belmont University in Nashville, TN. Layla is a Labrador Retriever who is known as "The Rehab Lab" because she loves helping in physical therapy and occupational therapy settings. They have also enjoyed visiting patients in oncology clinics and healthcare professionals in the ICU. Christi and Layla have researched the effects of therapy animals on student anxiety before exams.

Sue & Tucker

Sue is a pediatric physical therapist at The Therapy Center of Hendersonville in TN. Tucker is a Golden Retriever who comes to work with Sue every day. He loves to be a part of the therapy sessions with the children at the clinic. He helps them with the activities they are working on in therapy and is always ready to put a smile on everyone's face.

Chrissy & Norman

Chrissy is a neurologic physical therapist at Vanderbilt Pi Beta Phi Rehabilitation Institute. She has been partnering with Norman VI, a Labrador Retriever, since 2019. Norman graduated from Canine Companions for Independence (CCI) as a facility dog after completing two years of formal training. He was raised by volunteer puppy raisers at a military prison then returned to CCI headquarters for professional training. Norman is trained in over 50 commands to help patients with neurologic diagnoses participating in physical, occupational, and speech therapy.

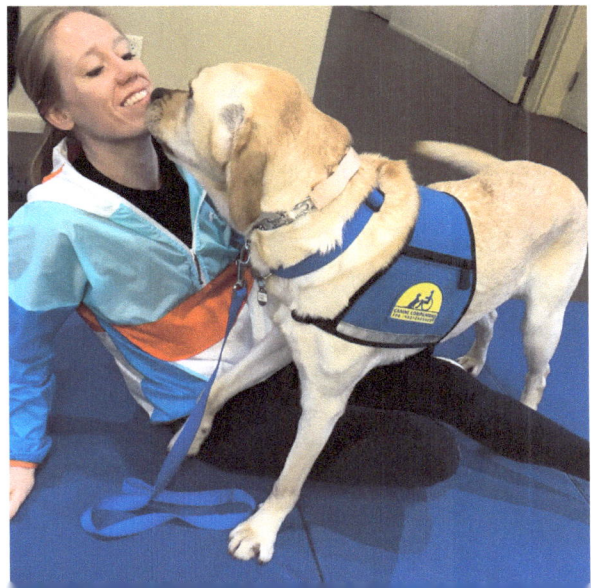

Dr. Will & Bodie

Dr. Will is a dentist at The Burkitt Center for Comprehensive Dentistry in Nolensville, TN. He is joined by Bodie, his Goldendoodle, who started visiting the office when he was a puppy. Bodie went through training to become a therapy dog to comfort patients during their dentist appointments. He loves to follow Dr. Will around the office to visit with patients and may even fall asleep on their lap. Bodie makes going to the dentist a little more fun.

Michelle & Swoosh

Swoosh is a Pomeranian who loves to bring a smile to people's faces. Michelle and Swoosh enjoy visiting nursing homes, schools, rehabilitation facilities, and the oncology clinic in the hospital. They were recently a part of a research study at Vanderbilt University Medical Center looking at the impact animals can have on children with cancer. Swoosh was awarded the Animal Medical Center's Top Dog Award in 2014.

Jenyfer & her therapy dogs

Jenyfer is a Certified Professional Dog Trainer, as well as an evaluator for the American Kennel Club. She has had eight registered therapy dogs, including Silver and Duncan whose stories were shared in this book. She recently served on the crisis response team with her dog, Alexis (pictured below). Together, they have traveled to various places to support those affected by natural disasters. Jenyfer has also visited many mental health centers and local domestic violence organizations.

Learn More

While the focus of this book was to educate others about how therapy dogs help people in healthcare settings, there are many other settings in which therapy dogs can visit. Therapy dogs also visit schools and universities, libraries, prisons, court rooms, funeral homes, disaster areas, and airports. To learn more about therapy dogs, including how to get your dog registered, visit:

WWW.THERAPYDOGHEALTHCARE.COM

References

Photo credits:

All photos in this book were used by permission.

- Page 4: Garrett Sapp, Charlotte Sapp, and Layla
- Page 7: Garrett Sapp and Layla
- Page 11: Layne Cagle, Chrissy Lugge, and Norman: photo by Steve Green, Vanderbilt University
- Page 16: Lillie Nuckols and Tucker
- Page 23: Ashley Rabuck, Katie Brelsford, and Maisy
- Page 24 & 25: Jon Jon Huddleston, Michelle Thompson, Mary Jo Gilmer, and Swoosh: photos by John Russell, Vanderbilt University
- Page 27 & 28: Mitchell Montalbano and Swoosh
- Page 30 & 31: Ms. Terri and Layla, Lori Day and Swoosh
- Page 32 & 33: Charlie Bertotti and Tucker
- Page 43: Katie Brelsford, Christa Schmieder, and Maisy
- Page 48: photo of Christi Williams & Layla by John Russell, Vanderbilt University
- Page 50: photo of Michelle Thompson and Swoosh by John Russell, Vanderbilt University
- Pages 3, 8, 15, & 18: photos by Kirby Brown
- Page 36, 40 & 41: photos by Katherine Beliveau Photography

References:

- An, H. J., & Park, S. J. (2021). Effects of animal-assisted therapy on gait performance, respiratory function, and psychological variables in patients post-stroke. *International Journal of Environmental Research and Public Health*, 18(11), 5818. https://doi.org/10.3390/ijerph18115818
- Cowfer, B., Akard, T.F., & Gilmer, M.J. (2021). Animal-Assisted interventions for children with advanced cancer: Child and parent perceptions. *Palliative Medicine Reports*, 2(1), 328-334. DOI: 10.1089/pmr.2021.0039

- Drah, H. (2022, February 18). 28 Most enticing pet therapy statistics (2022 Update). Retrieved 2022, from https://petpedia.co/pet-therapy-statistics/
- Gee, N. R., Mueller, M. K., & Curl, A. L. (2017). Human-Animal interaction and older adults: An overview. *Frontiers in Psychology*, 8, 1416. https://doi.org/10.3389/fpsyg.2017.01416
- Hedin, M. (2018, February 13). Therapy dogs may unlock health benefits for patients in hospital ICUs. The Hub. Retrieved 2022, from https://hub.jhu.edu/2018/02/12/therapy-dogs-could-help-icu-patients/
- le Roux, M. C., Swartz, L., & Swart, E. (2014). The effect of an animal-assisted reading program on the reading rate, accuracy and comprehension of grade 3 students: A randomized control study. *Child & Youth Care Forum*, 43(6), 655–673. https://doi.org/10.1007/s10566-014-9262-1
- Rodrigo-Claverol, M., Casanova-Gonzalvo, C., Malla-Clua, B., Rodrigo-Claverol, E., Jové-Naval, J., & Ortega-Bravo, M. (2019). Animal-Assisted intervention improves pain perception in polymedicated geriatric patients with chronic joint pain: A clinical trial. *International Journal of Environmental Research and Public Health*, 16(16), 2843. https://doi.org/10.3390/ijerph16162843
- Walker, H., Miller, M.C., Cowfer, B., Akard, TF., & Gilmer, M.J. (2021). Protocol of a pilot study of the effects of animal assisted interactions (AAI) on quality of life in children with life-threatening conditions and their parents. *International Journal of Palliative Care Nursing* 27(10), 524-530. DOI: 10.12968/ijpn. 2021.27.10.524
- Williams, C.L., Dagnan, E., Miner, K.M. & Sells, P. (2018). The effect of an animal-assisted intervention on physiological measures of stress and anxiety in graduate professional physical therapy students. *Open Access Library Journal*, 5: e4364. https://doi.org/10.4236/oalib.1104364
- Williams, C., Emond, K., Maynord, K., Simpkins, J., Stumbo, A. & Terhaar, T. (2018) An animal-assisted intervention's influence on graduate students' stress and anxiety prior to an examination. *Open Access Library Journal*, 5: e4831. https://doi.org/10.4236/oalib.1104831

ALL PROCEEDS FROM THE SALE OF
THIS BOOK WILL BE DONATED TO
LOCAL THERAPY DOG ORGANIZATIONS.
IT IS OUR HOPE THAT WITH THESE
DONATIONS, MORE PEOPLE WILL BE
ABLE TO REGISTER THEIR DOG AND
SERVE THEIR COMMUNITY BY
BRINGING JOY AND COMFORT TO
ALL THOSE IN NEED.

www.ingramcontent.com/pod-product-compliance
Lightning Source LLC
Chambersburg PA
CBHW060813090426
42737CB00002B/49